JOHANNE HANKO PH.D.

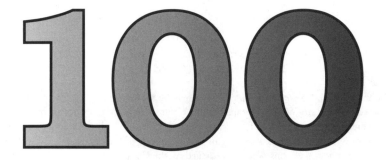

Learning Games
for Special Needs
with Music,
Movement, Sounds
and...Silence

Jessica Kingsley *Publishers*
London and Philadelphia

First published in 2012
by Jessica Kingsley Publishers
116 Pentonville Road
London N1 9JB, UK
and
400 Market Street, Suite 400
Philadelphia, PA 19106, USA

www.jkp.com

Library of Congress Cataloging in Publication Data
A CIP catalog record for this book is available from the Library of Congress

British Library Cataloguing in Publication Data
A CIP catalogue record for this book is available from the British Library

ISBN 978 1 84905 247 4

Printed and bound in Great Britain

Contents

Part I Developing Listening Skills

Part II Self and Environmental Awareness

Part III Sound and Tone Discrimination

Part IV Body Movement Control

Part V Breathing Control

Part VI Creative Thinking

Part VII Relaxation

About the Author

Johanne Hanko has been an educator and teacher of children and adults with special needs for over 20 years. She received her Bachelor's degree from Université du Québec in Montréal, her Master's degree from McGill University in Canada, specializing in education, special education, music and music therapy, and her Ph.D. from Bauhaus-Universität Weimar in Germany. She has been working in the education and rehabilitation of children with disabilities, and in capacity building and training of adolescents and adults with disabilities and war amputees toward their inclusion, rehabilitation, income generation and reintegration into society in various countries around North America, Asia, Africa and now South America. She has published numerous articles, books and training manuals for the United Nations and other organizations.

Realizing the necessity for children—and particularly children with special needs—to play and learn, she developed a number of learning games that were adapted according to the capacities and disabilities of children. These games have been successfully utilized in regular and special education teachers' training programs. Upon the request of these teachers, and due to the success of the games in terms of interest and learning results, she prepared a compilation of learning games which are presented in *100 Learning Games for Special Needs with Music, Movement, Sounds and…Silence*. All games in this book have been designed to suit the needs of children both with and without disabilities.

Explanation of Terms

Term	Definition
Activity room	The room or location where the activity is to take place (i.e. classroom, gymnasium, courtyard)
Beat	The basic rhythmic unit in a piece of music
Exceptions	The groups of players or the player that cannot participate in the game because of a specific limitation or disability
He/his/him	Also implies she/her/her Male gender is used throughout the book for ease of reading and understanding but implies male and female equally
Leader	The person in charge of guiding the group; in this case the parent, teacher, educator or the person organizing the game
Materials	Required items and props to be used during the games
Objectives	The goals intended to be attained and which are believed to be attainable by the child throughout the game
Percussion instrument	An instrument that is struck, shaken or scraped to produce sound (i.e. drum, cymbal, maracas)
Player	The child participating in the game regardless of age, gender, ability or disability
Rhythmic pattern	Recurring sequence of rhythm, i.e. ♩♩♫♩ ♩♩♫♩
Tempo	The speed at which a musical composition or an event is to take place
Tonal instrument	An instrument which produces specific tones or notes (i.e. piano, flute, xylophone)

Introduction

Children love to play, and games are one of the most efficient ways for a child to learn. Moreover, if a child suffers from some type of challenge or disability, learning can be more difficult and requires more time or additional practice prior to successfully achieving the task. What better way to teach or educate a child than through interesting, simple and specially adapted games. *100 Learning Games for Special Needs* uses music, movement, sounds and silence in various forms of activities as a stimulant toward the learning process of the child, targeting specific goals and answering special needs.

This book has been written to serve as a guide to teachers, parents and educators with the objective of teaching children the development of specific skills and abilities. The main objective of these games is to ensure that the learning process is an enjoyable and effortless exercise for the children to enjoy. The book is to be used as a guide for teaching and a tool for learning for children in preschool and elementary school, as well as for children with special educational needs who need to counter certain challenges. As a parent, a teacher or an educator, you will be able to enjoy, along with the children, fun games in pursuit of specific objectives: to develop learning skills, develop awareness of the self or of the immediate environment, develop sound and tone discrimination skills, learn how to better control the body, the breathing and speech, and develop creative thinking. Finally, the children will learn how to concentrate and relax.

These games should serve as a reference whereupon additional activities and learning games can be developed according to local traditions, customs and cultures as well as locally available materials and musical instruments.

Each game is presented on a single page. The title and illustration represent the principle of the game. *Age* refers to the age group most favorable for the game, although most games can be adapted for older or younger children. *Exception* is a specific warning of potential limitations for those children with disabilities or limitations for whom it will be impossible to play certain games. Most games, however, can be adapted for children with a physical or intellectual disability, and for children with visual or hearing impairments. *Materials* are then listed, allowing the leader to gather all items and props necessary to play the game.

The *Objectives* listed for each game provide just a few of the specific objectives; most games include a wide range of short- and long-term objectives that could be achieved.

The game is the description of the game which is kept as brief as possible; it should serve as a reference rather than a "recipe." Each leader should adapt the games according to personal style, skills and personality in order to make the games interesting and useful as learning tools. Several games include a number of *Variations* which show modifications of the same game, thus bringing the actual number of learning games in this book to 149.

Although some games seem to encourage competitiveness, this is not the purpose of the learning games. The fact is that competition often pushes a child a bit beyond his normal performance while trying to emulate his peers. In any case, it is necessary to ensure that the child completes the games successfully in order to avoid any deception, discouragement or frustration on the part of the child. The leader must always provide support and encouragement, ensuring teamwork and peer participation when in groups, and making sure the child develops specific skills to reach his full potential while enjoying the game.

I hope this book will be as useful to you as it has been for me, and that it will bring you the same enjoyment, successful results and gratification it has brought me over the years working in regular school settings and with children with special needs.

Materials Required for Activities

Note that some activities will need a number of the items on this list, while other activities will need just a few or none.

- paper bag (large grocery bag)
- noisy instruments or articles (bells, rattles, kitchen utensils, other noisy objects)
- blindfolds
- CD player/recorder, blank CDs, CDs of age-appropriate pop music, CDs of music from various countries
- feathers, drinking straws, silky paper (cardstock), cardboard rolls (e.g. empty toilet tissue or paper towel rolls)
- facial tissue (e.g. Kleenex®)
- colored pencils/crayons, large sheets of paper, scissors, glue, paper, cardboard, rubber bands, empty egg cartons, rope about 6 feet (2 meters) long
- chairs (variable number—one per player), large plastic hoops, cushions
- small table
- spotlights or flashlights
- silky scarves
- musical bingo cards (to be prepared by the leader), alphabet cards, animal picture cards
- blackboard/whiteboard, chalk/whiteboard marker

- black large garbage bag, books (or stacks of paper)
- newspaper
- long sticks and short sticks (wooden or plastic) approximately 8 inches and 12 inches (20 centimeters and 30 centimeters) long
- foam or very soft ball, large balls (the size of a soccer or basket ball)
- map of school or the training center (optional)
- access to video equipment
- stopwatch (chronometer)
- musical instruments: drum, mallet, xylophone, piano, flute, rhythm sticks, cymbal, small finger cymbals, tambourine, bells, resonating block, triangle, castanets, resonating bells, maracas

Note: Some of the above-mentioned items may not be available and can easily be substituted with similar readily available objects.

Target Groups

The learning games are suited for all children except when otherwise stated, in which case they can often be adapted.

Age groups

Most games are well suited to players between 4 and 12 years of age. Certain games can be adapted for younger players (4–8 years of age) and for older players (8–12 years of age), or according to physical and mental capabilities.

Note: Adolescents and adults with an intellectual disability can also benefit from many of the learning games.

Children targeted

- children with a physical disability
- children with an intellectual disability
- children with a hearing impairment
- children with a visual impairment
- children with autism
- children with emotional difficulties
- gifted and talented children
- regular preschool and kindergarten children
- regular elementary school children

Part I
Developing
Listening Skills

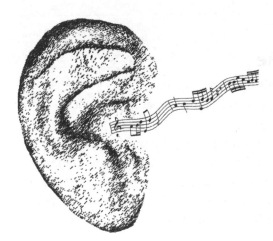

1

The Paper Bag

Age: For all ages.

Exception: Children with hearing impairment.

Materials: Paper bag, rattles and noisy items.

Objectives: Listening, body control, socialization.

The game

The group stands in a large circle.

Players must pass the empty paper bag around, not making any noise when handling the bag.

After the first round, put a rattle inside the bag.

After the second round, add another noisy item.

Every time a player makes noise with the bag or its contents, he is disqualified. The activity stops when only one player is left.

The game ends when all players have begun to control their movement.

2

The Little Dog Lost Its Collar

Age: For younger players.

Exception: Children with hearing impairment.

Materials: A collar with bells attached, blindfold.

Objectives: Listening, orientation, socialization.

The game

The group sits in a circle.

One player is blindfolded in the center of the circle (the little dog). Another player goes around outside the group sounding the collar; suddenly he stops and very quietly hands the collar to one of his peers sitting in the circle. The player now holding the collar, remaining seated, sounds the collar. Briefly, the leader asks the little dog to find its collar.

When the little dog finds its collar, he trades places.

The game ends when all players have been in the center as the little dog.

3

You're Getting Warmer

Age: For all players.

Exception: Can be adapted for children with hearing impairment.

Materials: Various musical instruments, blindfold.

Objectives: Listening, loud/soft discrimination, socialization.

The game

One player is blindfolded while other players sit around the activity room, each one holding one musical instrument.

The leader names another player whom the blindfolded player must find.

The player with a blindfold must find the other player by following the sound cues. By varying the intensity of the playing, the player with the blindfold will know if he is getting closer or farther away from the target (soft sound when far, very loud when very close). When the player is found, they change roles.

The game ends when all players have had a chance to be blindfolded.

Note: Instruments with high pitch, such as small cymbals or triangles, and/or those with low pitch, such as drums, can often be heard by children with a hearing impairment.

4

Human Obstacle

Age: For all players.

Exception: Can be adapted for children with hearing impairment.

Materials: Various small musical instruments, blindfold.

Objectives: Listening, reflexes, confidence in facing the unknown, socialization, self-control, environmental awareness.

The game

One player wears a blindfold and must walk across the activity room without touching any of the other players. The other players are scattered around the room (standing or sitting quietly), each holding a musical instrument but not moving. Every time the blindfolded player gets near someone, this person must alert him by playing his instrument. After the blindfolded player has reached the other side of the room, or after two or three minutes of wandering, change the player.

The game ends when all players have had a chance to be blindfolded.

Note: Instruments with high pitch, such as small cymbals or triangles, and/or those with low pitch, such as drums, can often be heard by children with a hearing impairment.

5

The Magic Wand

Age: For all ages.

Exception: Children with hearing impairment.

Materials: One stick, blindfold.

Objectives: Listening, tone discrimination, awareness of differences, self-control, socialization.

The game

The players sit in a circle.

The leader gives the "magic wand" (the stick) to a player (the magician) who sits in the center of the circle. A second player is chosen to blindfold the magician. The magician then calls "Who wants the magic wand?" The leader then designates (silently) which player is to answer "me." The magician must identify who has spoken. If he is correct, he gives the wand to the player who said "me" and blindfolds him. The blindfolded player is now the new magician.

The game ends when every player has been the magician.

Note: If players are found too easily, change the word "me" to a number or letter, or even change the tone of voice.

6

Loud and Soft

Age: For all ages.

Exception: Can be adapted for children with hearing impairment.

Materials: Cardboard, scissors, one (optional) musical instrument.

Objectives: Listening, loudness discrimination.

The game

The players cut out circles: three large and three small. The players are asked to listen to three sounds played by the leader. They must identify if the sound is loud or soft by placing the circles in the proper order with their size according to the intensity (loud = large circle, soft = small circle).

The game ends when all players understand the difference between loud and soft.

Variation 1: More sounds may be played according to the players' age or capabilities. A middle-sized circle may be added in order to increase the difficulty.

Variation 2: Players associate movement with the sounds; for example, they stand when the sound is loud, and they crouch when the sound is soft.

Variation 3: One player places the circles on the floor in random order. Players are asked to clap their hands according to the size of the circle: loud for a large circle and soft for a small circle.

Note: Instruments with high pitch, such as small cymbals or triangles, and/or those with low pitch, such as drums, can often be heard by children with a hearing impairment.

7

Short and Long

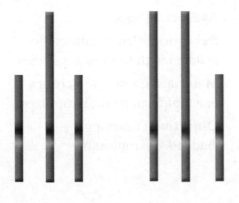

Age: For all ages.

Exception: Children with hearing impairment.

Materials: Three long sticks, three short sticks, one cymbal.

Objectives: Listening, time awareness.

The game

Players are asked to listen to three sounds played by the leader and determine their length. The leader plays the cymbal and lets it resonate for a long sound. For short sounds, the hand stops the resonance of the cymbal.

Players must then choose the stick according to the length of the sound that they heard.

The game ends when all players understand the meaning of long and short sounds.

Variation: The number of sticks can be increased according to the capability and age of the players.

8

The King and the Thief

Age: For all ages.

Exception: Children with hearing impairment.

Materials: Blindfold, rattle.

Objectives: Listening, socialization, spatial orientation, body control.

The game

Players are sitting in a circle.

One player is chosen as the king of silence. He is blindfolded and the rattle is placed at his feet. The leader chooses a thief who will try to steal the treasure (the rattle) without making any noise. The king must try to catch the thief by tagging him. When he finds him, the thief then becomes the king.

The game ends when every player has been the thief and the king.

9

Cat and Mouse

Age: For younger players.

Exception: Can be adapted for children with hearing impairment.

Materials: Drum or other percussion instrument.

Objectives: Listening, body movement control, facial expression, socialization.

The game

Players are spread throughout the activity room. They are all mice except for one who is in the middle, the cat. When the leader plays the instrument quickly and regularly, all the mice run. The cat cannot move; it watches and listens. When the leader taps the instrument very slowly, the mice stop moving and the cat moves in large steps toward the mice to try to catch one. When a mouse is caught, this player then becomes the cat.

The game ends when every player has been the cat.

Variation: The cat may be blindfolded.

Note: Instruments with high pitch, such as small cymbals or triangles, and/or those with low pitch, such as drums, can often be heard by children with a hearing impairment.

10

Musical Rings

Age: For all ages.

Exception: None (for children with hearing impairment, rock music with a heavy bass can be heard or felt).

Materials: Large plastic hoops (can be replaced by chairs, cushions, etc.), CD player, CDs.

Objectives: Listening, body movement control, socialization.

The game

Plastic hoops that are large enough to allow a player to stand or sit in are spread throughout the activity room; there is one hoop fewer than there are players. Players dance around the hoops to the music while the music is playing (the players must not touch or enter the hoops); they must move around all of the rings and not stay near just one hoop.

When the music stops, each player must jump into one hoop and sit down. The player left without a hoop is out. One hoop is then removed. The game goes on until there is only one player sitting in a hoop. The winner is then in charge of the music for the others to start a new game.

The game ends when each player has had a chance to be in charge of the music.

11

How Many Sounds Do You Hear?

Age: For all ages.

Exception: Children with hearing impairment.

Materials: Different musical instruments, paper, colored pencils.

Objectives: Listening, concentration, discrimination.

The game

The group sits with a sheet of paper and a colored pencil. Each player is asked to draw a square and divide it into four equal boxes. The leader, out of view, plays one, two or three sounds on different instruments. The player must recognize how many sounds were played and draw the same number of flowers in one of the boxes.

The game ends after repeating a few times when the concept of number of sounds is well understood.

Variation: Increase the number of sounds.

12

Do You Recognize Me?

Age: For all ages.

Exception: Can be adapted for children with visual or hearing impairment.

Materials: Paper, scissors, song pictures (explained below), glue, one rhythmic musical instrument such as a drum.

Objectives: Listening, rhythm discrimination, transfer of knowledge, association of ideas, fine motor skills.

The game

The group is given a sheet of paper with pictures representing four well-known children's songs. These pictures usually represent the main character of the song. The leader will sing each song with the players while showing the corresponding picture to make sure each player makes the correct picture/song association. The leader will then play the rhythm (not the melody) of the song on the percussion instrument. The player must recognize the song, cut out the picture and glue it on a blank sheet of paper. The game goes on until the rhythms of each song have been heard at least twice. The game ends when all four songs have been recognized.

Note 1: For children with a visual impairment, song illustrations can be cut out in advance or marked for cutting, offering different shapes for them to recognize.

Note 2: Instruments with high pitch, such as small cymbals or triangles, and/or those with low pitch, such as drums, can often be heard by children with a hearing impairment.

13

What Time Is It?

Age: For younger players.

Exception: Can be adapted for children with visual or hearing impairment.

Materials: Pencil, paper, triangle or another "sounding" instrument.

Objectives: Listening, body/eye coordination, counting, telling time.

The game

The group sits in front of four clocks printed on a sheet of paper (players can be asked to draw them). These clocks already have the minute hand on the 12, but the hour hand is missing.

The leader will play a number of sounds on an instrument. The player must draw the little hand on the correct number.

The game ends when all four clocks have been completed.

Note 1: For children with a visual impairment, the numbers and minute hand should be readable by touch.

Note 2: Instruments with high pitch, such as small cymbals or triangles, and/or those with low pitch, such as drums, can often be heard by children with a hearing impairment.

14

It's My Move

Age: For all ages.

Exception: Children with hearing impairment.

Materials: Musical instruments.

Objectives: Listening, discrimination, socialization, self-control.

The game

Each player is asked to team up with a partner. The leader selects three teams. Each team picks out one instrument (they must all be different), and one member of each team goes to hide in a different corner of the activity room in order not to be seen by his partner. All players are asked to play simultaneously yet independently of one another's tunes. The teammate must move only upon hearing his partner's instrument and stop when the sound stops. When he meets his partner, they switch places.

The game ends when all players have had a turn playing an instrument.

Note: If there are no hiding places, blindfolds can be used.

15

What Is That Strange Sound?

Age: Not for very young players.

Exception: Children with hearing impairment.

Materials: Five different musical instruments.

Objectives: Listening, discrimination, imagination.

The game

Five very different musical instruments are hidden in the activity room. A player sits with his back to the group and listens. The leader selects a player to play one of the five instruments in an unusual manner and return to the place he was sitting. The first player must then turn around, identify the instrument and play the same instrument in the same manner. If he achieves this, then he is the one who will select the player to play the next instrument. If not, he goes back to his place and awaits another chance. The player who played the instrument last then sits with his back to the group to listen. The leader selects the next player to play.

The game ends when all players have played an instrument and have tried to recognize the instrument played.

16

The Right Sequence

Age: For all ages.

Exception: Children with hearing impairment.

Materials: Familiar items that make peculiar sounds.

Objectives: Listening, memory, thought organization, imagination.

The game

Players sit facing the wall so they cannot see the leader. The leader chooses three to five different objects to make sounds (longer sequences for older players). For example, he may shake keys, shut the door, shuffle paper and move a chair. The player who thinks he can repeat these sounds in the same sequence is asked to do so. If he is right, he can then invent the next sequence.

The game ends when all players have invented one sequence.

Variation: Played the same as above except using musical instruments.

17

The Sound Circle

Age: For younger players.

Exception: Can be adapted
for children with hearing
or visual impairment.

Materials: A drum.

Objectives: Listening,
observation, discrimination of
loud and soft, socialization.

The game

One player stands in the middle of the group holding a drum while other
players stand in a fairly large circle surrounding him. There is space in front
of and behind the player with the drum. The player with the drum is asked to
play the instrument; if he plays loud, the circle of the group gets bigger; if he
plays soft, the circle gets smaller. The player plays the drum until he starts to
understand that he is controlling the size of the circle around him.

   The game ends when every player has had the opportunity to be in the
middle.

Variation: An additional player outside of the circle takes turns playing the
drum or another instrument with the player in the middle.

Note 1: The fact that the player is standing or sitting inside the circle rather
than outside will make him physically realize the difference between the sizes
of the circle. If a player is sitting outside, this player can make a point of
"squeezing" the player in the middle when the circle gets small.

Note 2: For children with a hearing impairment, the player in the middle with the drum should emphasize the movements. Large movements signify a large circle and small movements signify a small circle.

Notes 3: For children with a visual impairment, the other players must make noise with their feet following the sound of the drum in order for the player in the middle to hear the sound of the circle closing in or getting further away.

18

The Key Sound

Age: For all ages.

Exception: None.

Materials: A few different instruments.

Objectives: Listening, observation, self-control.

The game

Players stand facing the leader. The leader faces the players and has two different instruments. It is determined that one of these instruments is the secret "key sound." Only upon hearing (or seeing played) this key sound can players comply with the request associated with the key sound.

For example, the two instruments are the drum and the bell. The key sound is determined as the bell. The leader sounds the bell followed by the request "raise your hands"; the players must comply. The leader sounds the bell again and says lift one foot; the players comply. The leader sounds the drum and says "jump"; players must remain motionless. (A penalty can be given to those who moved without the proper key sound.) Players who understand the game well may, in turn, become the leader. The game ends when all players have had a chance to lead the game.

Variation 1: Same as above but with more than two instruments.

Variation 2: Same as above but without seeing the instruments.

Variation 3: Same as above but using a tonal instrument, in which case a specific note would be predetermined as the key sound. In this case, for older players, initially use faraway intervals and gradually reduce.

Note: Instruments with high pitch, such as small cymbals or triangles, and/or those with low pitch, such as drums, can often be heard by children with a hearing impairment.

19

Confusing the Singer

Age: For all ages.

Exception: Children with hearing impairment.

Materials: None.

Objectives: Listening, concentration, socialization.

The game

A player is asked to sing one or two bars of a very easy and familiar song. Another player tries to confuse the singer by singing different songs simultaneously. If after one minute the singer has still not made any mistakes, change both players. If the second player manages to confuse the singer, he then becomes the singer, and another player is chosen to confuse.

The game ends when all players have been the singer.

Note: The time allowed to confuse the singer can be increased or decreased depending on the players' capabilities.

20

I'm Going to Catch You

Age: For all ages.

Exception: Children with hearing impairment.

Materials: One chair for each player, blindfold.

Objectives: Listening, concentration, orientation, socialization.

The game

Players sit on chairs, in a circle. The leader verbally assigns a different number to each player. One player is blindfolded and stands in the center. The leader chooses two numbers. The two players given these numbers must change chairs without making any sound, and without being touched by the blindfolded player in the center. They must not move outside of the circle of chairs. The one that gets touched takes the blindfold.

The game ends when everybody has had a turn in the center.

21

The Musical Dance

Age: For all ages.

Exception: None.

Materials: CD player, pop or rock music CDs with accentuated rhythm.

Objectives: Listening, attention, self/body control, rhythm development, socialization.

The game

Players dance to the music, following the rhythm. When the music stops, they must become like statues in whatever position they are in; if they move after the music stops, they are out. The game stops when one dancer is left. He can then be in charge of stopping the music for the next round.

Repeat several times to ensure that players control their movement and can instantly stop moving.

The game ends when all players have had a chance to stop the music.

22

Follow the Beat

Age: For all ages.

Exception: Children with hearing impairment.

Materials: Drum, mallet, cymbal, gong (optional).

Objectives: Listening, discrimination, discipline.

The game

One player holds a drum and plays a regular beat. Players are required to move according to the beat of the drum:

- *Walk* on slow beat, following each beat.
- *Run* on very fast beat.
- Next add a cymbal to *walk backwards*.
- Then add a gong to *jump*.

The game ends when all players have had a chance to play the instruments.

Part II
Self and Environmental Awareness

23

I Know My Body

Age: For younger players.

Exception: None.

Materials: None.

Objectives: Self-awareness, body discovery, coordination.

The game

Players are asked to walk around the activity room. The leader calls out one part of the body. The players stop walking and start moving only that part of the body (e.g. head, arm, foot, finger).

The game ends when all parts of the body are well understood.

Variation: The players follow the beat of the drum while walking and moving the required part of the body.

24

Shadow Dancing

Age: For all ages.

Exception: Children with visual impairment.

Materials: Bright lights (spotlight), blank wall.

Objectives: Body awareness, contrast awareness (large/ small), socialization.

The game

Players lie down in front of a blank wall. All lights are turned off except for a spotlight aiming directly at the wall behind the players.

- Lying on the floor, players raise their hands in the air so that they see only their hands in the shadow. Make different figures.

- Do the same with the feet.

- Do the same with the whole body.

- Dance all together.

- Dance individually.

- Dance two by two.

- Make a sculpture in groups of two, three, etc.

- Make a sculpture all together.

- Check contrasts of large and small using distance from the wall (close = small, far = large).

The game ends when all players understand the shadows.

25

Know Your Instruments

Age: For all ages.

Exception: Can be adapted for children with visual impairment.

Materials: Paper and colored pencils/crayons.

Objectives: Self-awareness, knowledge, discrimination between sound production and reproduction, socialization, self-confidence.

The game

The player is asked to draw five musical instruments he knows. He then presents his drawings to the group and explains the instruments. There should be discussions on the various musical instruments, their differences, and how they differ from music production/reproduction systems such as radio, TV and stereo systems.

The game ends when all players understand the difference between sound production and reproduction.

Note: For children with a visual impairment, the player describes his drawing orally and then explains each instrument.

26

Know Your Musical World

Groups	Songs	Musical instruments

Age: For older players.

Exception: None.

Materials: Paper, pencil, alphabet cards.

Objectives: Spelling, real-life application, environment awareness, socialization.

The game

The group is divided into teams of three or four. Each team receives a sheet of paper and pencil. The sheet is to be divided into three columns: the first column is for groups, the second column is for songs and third column is for musical instruments. Using alphabet cards, one player pulls a card. Each team then has one minute to write all the groups, songs and musical instruments starting with this letter. Afterwards, findings are read to the group and discussed. Each correct answer (including correct spelling) earns one point. The group with the most points wins.

The game ends when several groups have scored the most points.

27

Will You Be My Guide?

Age: Not for very young players.

Exception: Can be adapted for children with visual impairment.

Materials: Blindfolds.

Objectives: Responsibility, auditory awareness, socialization, orientation.

The game

The group is divided into pairs. One teammate is blindfolded, the other is the guide. Both walk carefully around the school. The guide is responsible for the security of the teammate. After ten minutes, change roles.

The game ends when all players have been both blindfolded and the guide.

Note: In case all participants are children with visual impairment, the activity must be closely supervised by trained leaders to ensure the security of the players.

28

My Body, the Sound Machine

Age: For younger players.

Exception: Children with hearing impairment.

Materials: None.

Objectives: Self-assurance, environmental awareness, imagination.

The game

In teams of three or four, players must find all the different sounds they can make with their body.

Each team then presents its findings to the others.

The game ends when all teams have presented their body sounds.

Variation 1: Find the different sounds they can make with external objects such as: slamming the door, dropping a pencil, tearing paper.

Variation 2: Identify the different sounds heard in the environment, such as: motor vehicles, dogs barking, birds and wind.

29

How Many People Behind Me?

Age: For older players.

Exception: Children with hearing impairment.

Materials: None.

Objectives: Listening, concentration, environmental awareness.

The game

Players sit in the activity room. One player is standing with his back to the others. In complete silence, one by one, players will come and stand behind the one turning his back. The player must try to listen and say how many are standing behind him.

The game ends when every player has tried to guess the number of players behind him.

Variation: Blindfold the player to minimize his peripheral vision.

30

What Has Been Changed?

Age: For all ages.

Exception: Children with visual impairment.

Materials: None.

Objectives: Environmental awareness, observational skills, memory, socialization.

The game

Players sit with their backs to a wall. One player stands in front of the others and allows everybody to visually check him, verifying details. He then goes outside the activity room and changes something on himself (e.g. pushes up a sleeve, puts sweater inside out, changes hair style). He then comes back in and the others try to discover what has been changed. The player that works it out wins and trades placcs.

The game ends when every player has had a chance to change something on himself.

31

It Sounds Like This

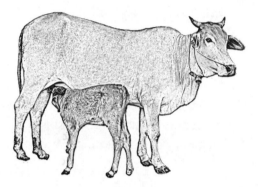

Age: For younger players.

Exception: Can be adapted for children with visual impairment.

Materials: Animal picture cards, different instruments.

Objectives: Imagination, body awareness, physical abilities, observation, thought association.

The game

A player is asked to select an animal card and imitate the sound of this animal. Another player is asked to choose an instrument that he thinks corresponds to the animal, and explain in which ways there is a relationship (e.g. cow-horn, bird-whistle).

The game ends when all players have had a chance to select the animal and to choose a corresponding instrument and explain it.

Note: For children with visual impairment, the cards must allow the player to recognize the animal by touch.

32

I Move Like a(n) _____ (Animal)

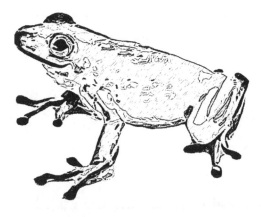

Age: For all ages.

Exception: Can be adapted for children with visual impairment.

Materials: Animal picture cards.

Objectives: Observation, imagination, socialization, awareness, means of locomotion.

The game

Scatter cards with pictures of different types of animal throughout the activity room. There should be at least one card per player. Each player sits near a picture card, looks at it and, upon the leader's signal, must move like that animal in order to reach another card; he must try to find a card where there are not many people. Upon reaching that card, the player must change his way of moving according to this new animal.

The game ends when the players have moved to each of the cards.

Variation 1: I Move Like a(n) _____ (Insect)

Variation 2: I Move Like _____ (Cartoon Character)

Note: For children with visual impairment, the cards must allow the player to recognize the animal by touch, for example by recognizing the shape or reading the name in Braille.

33

A Walk in the Jungle

Age: For all ages.

Exception: None.

Materials: Ropes about 6 feet (2 meters) long. One rope per six players.

Objectives: Environmental awareness, consciousness of levels, patterns, speed, socialization.

The game

With everyone sitting on the floor, the leader explains that they will take a walk in the jungle. The group brainstorms as to what can be encountered in the jungle—animals, plants, water, dangers, insects, type of environment. The players are then grouped in teams of five or six. They all stand one behind the other holding a rope with one hand. The player in front is the chief. The leader will announce what is happening and the chief will have to walk according to instructions, with the others imitating the chief (e.g. walking on very hot sand, walking in a very low cavern, creeping very slowly so as not to disturb the animals). The chief then goes to the end of the rope and the player now at the front becomes the chief.

The game ends when every player has had a chance to be the chief.

Part III
Sound and Tone Discrimination

34

I Know Where It Comes From

Age: For all ages.

Exception: Children with hearing impairment.

Materials: Blindfolds for each player, one instrument for each player—all very different.

Objectives: Listening, tone discrimination, attention, socialization.

The game

The group of players sits in a circle. Each player holds a different musical instrument. One player is in the center wearing a blindfold. The leader gives the name of the instrument that must be recognized. At the signal, all the players start playing simultaneously. Just by listening, the player in the center must find where the instrument is without touching it. When he finds it, he trades places with the player of that instrument. If he gets it wrong, he stays in the center until he has located the instrument.

The game ends when each player has had a chance to be in the center.

35

Which Instrument Is Missing?

Age: For all ages.

Exception: Children with hearing impairment.

Materials: One instrument for each player—all very different.

Objectives: Listening, tone discrimination, memory, socialization.

The game

Each player has a different instrument. One player is selected by the leader to go in front of the group and to listen carefully to each instrument, one by one. He then turns his back and closes his eyes. The leader quietly selects one player who will not play and gives the signal for all the others to play simultaneously. The player with his back turned must say which instrument is not being played. If he finds it, he trades places with the non-player. If he misses, he tries to guess again.

The game ends when each player has had a chance to go in the middle.

36

Listen to the Clues

Age: For all ages.

Exception: Can be adapted for children with hearing impairment or visual impairment.

Materials: Anything that can be used as an obstacle (chair, table, books), two to four musical instruments with different tones, blindfolds.

Objectives: Listening, tone discrimination, spatial orientation, concentration, memory, socialization.

The game

Obstacles are placed around the activity room. In teams of two, one teammate is blindfolded, the other is the guide. The guide uses musical sounds to direct the blindfolded player through an obstacle course. Specific sounds must be established before starting.

For example, with two instruments: drum = turn right; sticks = turn left.

The blindfolded player must listen and follow the directions. When completed, change roles.

The game ends after each player has been blindfolded.

Variation: Use four instruments:

Drum = turn right   Maracas = walk backward

Sticks = turn left   Bell = walk forward

Note 1: For children with visual impairment, the leader can play the instruments.

Note 2: Instruments with high pitch, such as small cymbals or triangles, and/or those with low pitch, such as drums, can often be heard by children with hearing impairment.

37

Musical Bingo

Age: For all ages.

Exception: Children with visual impairment or hearing impairment.

Materials: Bingo cards with musical instrument illustrations (to be prepared by the leader or the players).

Objectives: Listening, sound and tone discrimination, concentration, eye/ear association, socialization.

The game

The leader hides to play one instrument after another, and the players must put a token (or small piece of paper) on the illustration of the instrument they have heard, if it appears on their bingo card. The first player to have a straight or diagonal line or all four corners is the winner; the winner gets to play the instruments for the next round. It is recommended that the leader play the instruments in front of the players the first few times. Then the leader can play the instruments so the players cannot see them.

The game ends after there have been a few different winners, when the leader knows the players understand the sounds and the associated picture.

Variation 1: Replace sounds of musical instruments with daily living sounds.

Variation 2: Replace sounds of musical instruments with sounds of nature.

38

The Sound Chart

Drum	Wood block	Triangle	Flute
Maracas		Spoons	Cymbals
Bell			Castanets
Tambourine	Cow bell		Rhythm sticks

Age: For all ages.

Exception: Children with visual impairment.

Materials: Blackboard, chalk, 10–12 different musical instruments.

Objectives: Listening, reading skills, concentration, socialization.

The game

Ten to twelve different musical instruments are presented by the teacher and shown to the group.

The leader then draws a chart on the board containing 16 boxes (four by four). Players are asked in turn to name one of the instruments (the same instrument cannot be named more than two or three times). The names are written (or drawn for children who cannot read) in the boxes. When all the boxes are filled in, the leader checks for repeated instruments and keeps only one of the same instrument by erasing the other(s). These empty boxes will become rests or silence. Each player then selects one instrument. Following the leader who is pointing at the board, box by box, the player plays his instrument (one beat) when the leader shows this specific instrument. Everything must be done in rhythm. When pointing to the empty box, nobody must play.

The game ends after several repetitions when everybody is playing smoothly and in tempo.

39

The Secret

Age: For all ages.

Exception: None.

Materials: None.

Objectives: Evaluation, synchronization, socialization.

The game

Divide the group into two teams. The leader gives secret instructions to one of the teams to do something specific during their choreography or dance (e.g. jump or clap hands). The other team must find out what that secret is. Once the secret has been identified, the second team performs its secret move. Each player in each team invents a secret to present to the other team.

The game ends when all players have invented a secret.

Variation: Can be done while dancing to music.

40

High and Low

Age: For all ages.

Exception: Can be adapted for children with hearing impairment.

Materials: Two large carpets in the room.

Objectives: Listening, concentration, pitch discrimination.

The game

Two carpets are spread in the activity room: one carpet for high pitch, the other for low pitch. The leader plays the piano (or any other tonal instrument). When the leader plays in the high range, players go to the high-range carpet and dance while standing. When the leader plays in the low range of the piano, players go to the low-range carpet and dance while crouching.

Once players understand the game, they can be asked to play the instrument.

The game ends when all players fully understand the difference between high and low without hesitation.

Note: As children with a hearing impairment can often hear vibrations, the leader can start by asking them to place their ear on the piano in order to recognize the difference in vibrations between high and low. He can then play the piano with exaggerated movements so that players can see clearly when high notes are being played and when low notes are being played. An alternative to the piano is the xylophone, which shows difference in pitch with bars of different lengths.

41

The Giant and the Boy

Age: For younger players.

Exception: None.

Materials: None.

Objectives: Facial expression, vocal chords exercise, self-confidence, role playing, courage.

The game

Half the group are labelled as giants and the other half are little boys. Giants are perceived as strong and powerful while little boys are small and frightened. When the giants move toward the little boys, the little boys are frightened and run away. After a few minutes, players change roles.

The game ends when each player has been a little boy and a giant.

Note: Although this game appears simple in essence, it allows the shyer players to become strong and powerful for a few seconds or minutes to build self-confidence.

42

Dances of All Colors

Age: For all ages.

Exception: None.

Materials: Music CDs from different countries.

Objectives: Listening, imagination, knowledge acquisition, new body movements.

The game

Players listen to music from different parts of the world. With the help of the leader, they must try to identify the country. The leader explains the particulars of the country and of the instruments that are heard. Players are asked to dance the way they imagine people do in those countries. The number of countries visited will depend on the knowledge of the leader.

The game ends when several countries have been presented and discussed.

43

Hide and Listen

Age: For all ages.

Exception: Children with hearing impairment.

Materials: Blindfold.

Objectives: Listening, spatial orientation, self-esteem.

The game

One player sits in the middle of the activity room with a blindfold. All the others hide somewhere in the room; they must stay where they are. The leader chooses one player to make a sound (e.g. scratching, growling, squeaking). The player with the blindfold must find the source of the sound. Once found, this player is blindfolded and the others hide again. The leader selects another player to make the noise.

The game ends when all players have had a chance to be blindfolded.

44

I'm a Conductor

Age: For all ages.

Exception: Children with visual impairment.

Materials: Xylophone or other musical instruments.

Objectives: Listening, self-control, initiative, awareness of contrasts, power of decision, attention, movement control.

The game

All players have an instrument. They can play any notes but must play only when they receive the signal from the conductor.

- They must play loudly when the conductor indicates loud (by raising arms).

- They must play softly when the conductor indicates soft (by lowering arms).

- They must play quickly when the conductor indicates quick (by quick movements).

- They must play slowly when the conductor indicates slow (by slow movements).

Players take turns becoming the conductor.

The game ends after each player has been the conductor and understands the contrasts.

45

Who Said That?

Age: For all ages.

Exception: Children with hearing impairment.

Materials: Musical instruments.

Objectives: Listening, concentration, intensity discrimination, socialization.

The game

Players sit back to back in two rows. Each player has an instrument. Each instrument is repeated in the second row but not in the same order. One player plays a rhythmic pattern on his instrument; the player with the *same instrument* in the second row repeats *exactly the same rhythm*. A second player from the first row plays a rhythmic pattern that is repeated in the second row by the same instrument. And so on.

The game ends when each player has invented at least one rhythmic pattern.

46

Listening to the School

Age: For all ages.

Exception: Children with hearing or visual impairment.

Materials: School map, colored pencils or crayons.

Objectives: Listening, intensity discrimination, self-control.

The game

The leader makes copies or draws a map of the school (older players can be asked to draw the map themselves). Players are divided into teams of two or three teammates. Each team is given a copy of the map. By using the map, players walk around the school very quietly and listen to the level of noise in each area of the school. They color the map according to what they hear: red = loud, yellow = medium, green = silent.

Players return to the class after they have finished coloring the school map. All compare drawings and discuss any differences.

The game ends after all players have had a chance to present and discuss their colored map.

47

Battle of the Musical Instruments

Age: For all ages.

Exception: Children with hearing impairment.

Materials: Newspaper, chairs.

Objectives: Socialization, memory, concentration, reflexes.

The game

All the players sit on chairs in a circle with their hands on their knees. Each player selects the name of a musical instrument (all different). The names of the instruments are written on the board. (Depending on age, the name of the player may or may not be written beside the name of the instrument.)

One player stands in the middle with a loosely rolled-up newspaper. The game starts when the leader gives the name of one musical instrument. The player with the newspaper must use it to touch the hands of the player who has selected this instrument. To avoid getting touched, this player must name another instrument, and the player with the newspaper must then find this new player to try to touch him before he has a chance to name yet another instrument. If the player with the newspaper taps the other player before he can name another instrument, the other player then becomes the player in the middle and takes the newspaper.

The game ends when all players have had a chance to be in the middle with the newspaper.

48

Who Does This Item Belong To?

Age: For all ages.

Exception: None.

Materials: Large bag or box.

Objectives: Imagination, socialization, self-confidence.

The game

All players sit along the wall. Every player puts a personal item (such as a shoe) in a large bag. One player then sits in front, his back to the others. An object is drawn by one of the players along the wall. The one sitting in front gives a command in order for the owner of the object to get back his belongings, without knowing who it belongs to (the object can also be his own). All commands must be artistically oriented (sing a song, dance, play an instrument). The player must accept the command (not lasting more than 30 seconds) in order to get back his belongings. He then replaces the player in front and can give the command for the next drawn item.

The game ends when each player has had a chance to give one command.

49

I Can Hear You

Age: For all ages.

Exception: Children with hearing impairment.

Materials: None.

Objectives: Listening, tone discrimination within others, socialization, orientation, concentration.

The game

In teams of two, players stand in two rows face to face and far apart. Players in the first row close their eyes. Players in the second row change places. They then stand still and all at the same time call the name of their partner. Players from the first row must follow the voice while keeping their eyes closed. Only the ones with their eyes closed can move. When the teammates have all found each other, the players change roles.

The game ends when all players have had a chance to be found and to look for their teammate.

Variation 1: Those with their eyes closed and the callers can all move.

Variation 2: The callers can whisper.

Variation 3: The callers play a musical instrument.

50

Follow the Wanderer

Age: For all ages.

Exception: Children with visual impairment.

Materials: Various instruments.

Objectives: Association of sound and movement, concentration, body awareness, rhythm, socialization.

The game

One player walks through the activity room while the others follow the movement on their instrument—one step/one beat (fast, slow, high, low…).

The game ends when each player has wandered through the room.

Variation: One player plays an instrument while the others follow the movement with their body.

Note: It is impressive to see some children with severe physical difficulties walking quite well while following the beat of a drum, and forgetting their disability for a moment while concentrating on the beat (some even forget their crutches!).

51

What Is That Sound?

Age: For all ages.

Exception: Children with hearing impairment.

Materials: Different musical instruments.

Objectives: Listening, tone discrimination, concentration.

The game

Musical instruments are placed where the players cannot see them (behind a curtain, under a table, etc.). The number of instruments will depend on the age and mental capabilities of the children. Usually between 6 and 12 instruments are used. The leader plays one instrument. The player who thinks he knows which instrument he heard is selected to go and play that same instrument. If he is correct, he replaces the leader to choose and play the instrument for the group to recognize. If the player is wrong, he goes back to his place.

The game ends when all players have had a chance to select and play an instrument.

52

You Didn't See Me Move!

Age: For all ages.

Exception: Children with visual impairment.

Materials: None.

Objectives: Socialization, honesty, self-control, concentration, observation.

The game

The leader stands in front of the group with his back to them. The players stand side by side at the end of the activity room. The players must sneak up to the leader and touch him without being seen. A player may be seen in a different place but must never be seen moving. If a player is seen moving, he must go back to the starting point. If not, he advances until he reaches the leader. The leader can turn around at any time. When the leader turns around, everybody must stop moving completely. Once a player has reached the leader and touched him, this player then takes the place of the leader and the game starts again.

The game ends when every player has taken the place of the leader.

53

The Telephone

Age: For all ages.

Exception: None.

Materials: None.

Objectives: Concentration, memory, precision.

The game

Players sit in a straight line one behind the other; the number of players depends on the age and capabilities. The player sitting at the end of the line taps a rhythmic pattern (very short—two beats, or four beats for older players) on the back of the player sitting in front of him. The latter then plays it on the back of the player in front of him, and so on until it reaches the player sitting at the front. This player must then clap the rhythm with his hands or play it on a drum. If it is incorrect, the leader of the team must try to find where the mistake came from by going down the line. The player sitting in front then goes to the end of the line and invents a new pattern.

The game ends when all of the players have invented a pattern.

Variation: This game can be done as a race by separating the group into two teams. The leader gives the rhythm to the last player of each team and, upon the signal given by the leader, the players start tapping the rhythmic pattern on the back of the player in front of them. The first team in which the player at the front of the line claps the "correct" rhythmic pattern is the winner. If the rhythm is incorrect, the team must start again.

54

My Name Is

Age: For very young players.

Exception: None.

Materials: Rhythmic musical instruments.

Objectives: Rhythm development, socialization, speech development.

The game

Each player has an instrument and sits in a circle. Each player says his name in rhythm with the instrument (one syllable = one beat) and the others repeat it a few times.

The game ends when each player has said his name.

Variation: Add: "*My name is* Ma-ry" or "*My name is* Tom" said and played in rhythm:

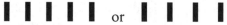

55

Playing on *My* Beat

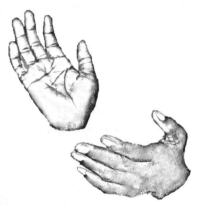

Age: For older players.

Exception: None.

Materials: None.

Objectives: Listening, concentration, coordination, socialization.

The game

The group is divided into two teams. Both teams together clap eight beats in regular rhythm while counting to eight in their head.

Then each team is told to clap their hands *only on a specific beat*. For example, first team on third beat, second team on sixth beat. Each team must always count all the beats in their head and only play on their beat.

The objective is to see if both teams can maintain the beat for two to three minutes. They must practice until they can do it. Then one person has to clap anywhere within the rhythm to try to confuse the others.

The game ends when players start to control the beat.

Variation 1: Divide the group into three teams and assign a third beat.

Variation 2: Divide the group into four teams and assign a fourth beat.

Variation 3: The beat can be played on an instrument.

56

Relaying the Beat

Age: For older players.

Exception: Children with hearing impairment.

Materials: None.

Objectives: Body movement control, synchronization, attention, memory, socialization, rhythm development.

The game

The group sits in a circle (on chairs or on the floor). Each player chooses the name of an instrument, which is written on a board. Each instrument must be different. A succession of movements is learned and repeated, such as: "Tap left hand on left knee," "right hand on right knee," "point left thumb over left shoulder," "right thumb over right shoulder." When the movement becomes natural, in a slow four-beat movement, the first player then starts naming his instrument when pointing the left thumb, and another player's instrument when pointing the right thumb. The word and the movement must be done simultaneously. The other player, upon hearing his instrument, must, on the first beat, start to tap his left knee, then tap his right knee, then say his instrument while raising his left thumb, and say another's player's instrument when raising his right thumb; this relays the game to another player. If there is a mistake, the player is out of the game or the game starts over. The next player must do the same as the first in naming a third player's instrument, and so on. A slow tempo is preferable at the beginning; it can then be accelerated as the number of mistakes decreases.

The game ends when all players understand the beat and are capable of accelerating the tempo.

Part IV
Body Movement Control

57

You Are My String Puppet

Age: Not for very young players.

Exception: Children with visual impairment.

Materials: None.

Objectives: Body control and awareness, socialization, relaxation, imagination.

The game

In teams of two, one player is a puppet and the other is a puppeteer. The puppeteers tie the puppets in the position they want using imaginary strings. The puppets cannot say or do anything except position themselves as the puppeteers position them. When the puppeteers are finished, upon the signal of the leader, the puppeteers cut the imaginary strings with imaginary scissors. All the puppets fall to the floor. Participants switch roles.

The game ends when all players have had a few turns at being puppeteers and puppets.

58

Playing a Role

Age: For all ages.

Exception: Children with visual impairment.

Materials: Paper, pencils.

Objectives: Body movement, coordination, self-control (no voice or sounds), socialization, role playing, reading skills.

The game

Simple two- to five-word sentences are written on small pieces of paper (e.g. I play violin; I am a happy boy; You are singing; That is a small dog). These sentences can be prepared by the participants or by the leader (depending on age and capabilities). Sentences can be restricted to specific areas of knowledge such as musical instruments, moods, animals and daily life situations. One player randomly chooses a paper, reads and remembers it in his mind and mimes the content. Others must figure out the meaning. The one who guesses correctly takes his place.

The game ends when all players have had a chance to mime.

Variation: For younger players, replace sentences with picture cards of animals, actions or other things that they can easily imitate.

59

Different Ways

Age: For all ages.

Exception: None.

Materials: None.

Objectives: Imagination, body movement control, self-awareness, transfer of knowledge.

The game

Each player, in turn, is asked to move across the activity room while demonstrating an unusual way of:

- walking
- then jumping
- then running
- and finally turning.

The same action cannot be done twice or imitated by other players.

The game ends when all players have had a chance to demonstrate several ways.

60

Which One Is Shorter?

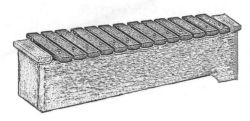

Age: For all ages.

Exception: None.

Materials: Xylophones—preferably one per person. Xylophones must be easy to take apart and reassemble.

Objectives: Body movement control, hand/eye coordination, notion of length.

The game

Each player sits with a xylophone. The player takes all of the bars off, one by one. He mixes the bars and has to put them back where they belong in the correct order, from longer to shorter.

Once the instrument is reassembled, the player can play the instrument.

The game ends when all players can easily dismantle the bars of the xylophone and put them back in the proper order.

61

Reflex Ball

Age: For all ages.

Exception: Children with visual impairment.

Materials: One very soft ball (sponge preferred).

Objectives: Self-control, coordination, motor skills, socialization.

The game

All players stand along a wall. They cross their arms. The leader throws or pretends to throw the ball. If the leader throws it to a player, this player must catch it and return it to the leader. No other players must unfold their arms. If the leader just pretends to throw it, none of the players can uncross their arms. Those who do are out. The winner is the last remaining player, who then gets to throw (or pretend to throw) the ball to his peers.

The game ends when all players have had the opportunity to throw the ball.

62

Follow Hands and Feet

Age: For all ages.

Exception: Can be adapted for children with visual impairment.

Materials: Paper, scissors.

Objectives: Coordination, organization, balance, body movement control.

The game

The leader and/or the players cut out paper hands and feet. These are then spread out on the floor of the activity room within reachable distances, thus creating a road made up of hands and feet. At the end of this road is a secret message. The players must walk using hands and feet as indicated, in order to read the message at the end of the road. The message can be as simple as "Have a nice day."

The game ends when every player has had a chance to read the message.

Variation: Organize as a race using either two roads or a stopwatch to see who is fastest.

Note: For children with a visual impairment, the hands and feet must be thick enough to be easily recognized by touch, and the message can be replaced by an item to be identified (e.g. a pencil or toy, or a message in Braille).

63

The Tightrope Walker

Age: For all ages.

Exception: None.

Materials: Large plastic garbage bag, scissors, miscellaneous objects to be used as obstacles (chairs, tables, books).

Objectives: Coordination, motor control, concentration.

The game

A line is made by cutting a long strip out of a large plastic garbage bag, 15–30 feet (5–10 meters) long and 2–3 inches (5–7 centimeters) wide. This line will go on the floor, over books, under tables, over chairs, etc. The length of the obstacle course depends on the size of the activity room. The obstacle course will be duplicated exactly to allow two players to walk simultaneously.

The race begins. The player must make sure his feet are always on the line. If he steps off of it, he must start from the beginning until he reaches the end of the path.

The game ends when all players can easily walk the tightrope.

Variation: If space is limited, a stopwatch can be used instead of the second path. In this case, if the player steps off the line, he must start again while the stopwatch continues. The player going through the course in the shortest time is the winner.

64

Mirror Dancing

Age: For all ages.

Exception: Children with visual impairment.

Materials: CD player, CDs with rhythmic music.

Objectives: Imagination, body movement control, physical abilities, rhythm, socialization.

The game

The leader dances in front of the group. Every player is a mirror. Players must imitate the exact movements of the leader. Then one player goes in front of the group, and the others are his mirrors.

The activity ends when each player has had the opportunity to be imitated.

65

Slow Motion Movies

Age: For all ages.

Exception: Children with visual impairment.

Materials: None.

Objectives: Self-control, movement control, facial expression, awareness of others, coordination, socialization.

The game

In pairs, the players are to become movie actors. They pretend to fight and receive their adversary's blows, without touching each other. They pretend they are hurt. Their actions mimic a slow motion movie.

The game ends when both "actors" are in good control of their movements.

66

Silent Dancing

Age: For all ages.

Exception: Can be adapted for children with hearing impairment.

Materials: None.

Objectives: Self-control, body movement control, socialization.

The game

Divide the group into two teams. The first team dances with no music and tries to make no sounds. The other team, along with the leader, listens for the subtle sounds made by the movements. Every time a sound is heard, the leader takes off one point. They must dance for two or three minutes (depending on the age of the players) without producing a single sound; after the required time is up, teams trade places. The team that loses the fewest points wins.

The game ends after it has been repeated a few times to allow the players to control their movements, and to allow each team to win a few times.

Note: For children with a hearing impairment, the leader can be the person to listen for sounds during the silent dancing so that the dancers can focus on controlling their movements.

67

Accentuation

Age: For all ages.

Exception: None.

Materials: One percussion instrument per player (e.g. drum, sticks).

Objectives: Body control, listening, concentration, rhythm control.

The game

Players sit in a circle, each holding a percussion musical instrument. All players should have the same instrument. A four-beat rhythm is chosen (like the one shown above). Each player must play one beat only; the first beat should be played much louder than the others. Rhythms can be as simple as four quarter notes (crotchets) or four equal beats. The first beat is played loudly by the first player, the second by the player next to him, the third by the third player and the fourth by the fourth player. Then the next player plays the first beat louder still, and so on. No player should play on the same beat twice (make sure the number of players is uneven). For older players, rhythmic patterns can be more complicated.

The game ends when players start feeling the strong beat and begin to play on time and in rhythm.

68

The Rhythmic Ball

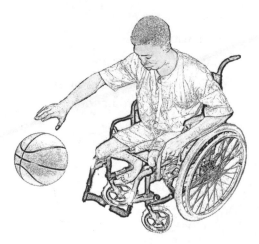

Age: For all ages.

Exception: Can be adapted for children with visual impairment.

Materials: One large ball.

Objectives: Body control, coordination, socialization.

The game

Players sit in a circle. The leader sits in the center holding a ball. The leader throws the ball to one of the players, who then throws it back. The leader then throws it to the next player, who throws it back, and so on. The ball must go around in a regular and controlled tempo. After the first round, the leader starts increasing the speed while maintaining a regular tempo. The player who misses the ball lies down on the floor (or loses one point). The game continues. If the players are very good, the ball can be thrown at random rather than in order.

The game ends when only one player is left or when the leader considers that the players have acquired a good control of the ball. The winning player can go in the center of the circle to throw the ball to the others.

The activity ends when all players have had a chance to throw the ball from the center.

Variation: A smaller ball can be used to increase the difficulty.

Note: For children with visual impairment, the name of the player can be said immediately before throwing the ball.

69

Catch It Before It Falls

Age: For all ages.

Exception: None.

Materials: Silky scarves.

Objectives: Body control, spatial orientation, coordination.

The game

Each player has a scarf. The leader announces that the scarf must be caught with a specific part of the body (e.g. head, right arm, left foot, face, back). The player is asked to place the scarf in a bundle in his hand and, on the leader's signal, to throw the scarf into the air. The scarf will then unfold itself in the air and the player must catch it with the chosen part of his body.

The game ends when several parts of the body have been used and players are becoming more skilled at catching the scarves.

Part V
Breathing Control

70

Feather Racing

Age: For all ages.

Exception: Children with visual impairment.

Materials: Very light feathers (one for each player; the leader should have extras).

Objectives: Air control, understanding of blowing/ suction principles, socialization, speech improvement.

The game

Players are on the floor, on their hands and knees, one beside the other. Each player has a feather in front of him. Players must blow the feather across the activity room at least 15 feet (5 meters) and blow it back to their starting point as quickly as possible. The first one back is the winner. If the group is large, players can work in pairs. If there is an odd number of players, one player can act as a referee and then trade places with another player.

The game ends when all players understand the blowing process.

Note 1: Each player must cross the finish line in whatever amount of time is needed (other players are asked to encourage any player having difficulties).

Note 2: Spare feathers are often necessary, especially with children with speech impairments, who will spit on the feather because of lack of control of the blowing process, making the feather unusable within a few minutes.

71

The Vacuum Race

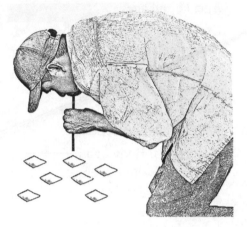

Age: For all ages.

Exception: Can be adapted for children with visual impairment.

Materials: Small drinking straws, onion skin paper cut into one inch (2.5 centimeter) square pieces.

Objectives: Coordination, breath control, tongue control, understanding of blowing/ suction principles, socialization, speech improvement.

The game

Players sit on the floor side by side. Each player is given a straw and seven pieces of thin paper. The player must use the straw for suction to hold the paper and take it to the other side of the activity room. After taking all seven pieces of paper, the player comes back and sits at the starting point. The first player to finish is the winner. If the group is large, players can work in pairs. If there is an odd number of players, one can act as a referee and then trade places with another player.

The game ends when all players understand the suction process.

Note 1: Each player must transfer all seven pieces of paper in whatever amount of time is needed (other players are asked to encourage any player having difficulties).

Note 2: In some cases, it may be necessary to use a glass of water to help understand the suction principle that is then to be repeated in transporting the paper.

Note 3: Spare papers are often necessary, especially with children with speech impairment, who will spit on the paper because of lack of control of the suction process, making the paper unusable within a few minutes.

Note 4: Allow children with a visual impairment to touch the paper.

72

Rolling Away

Age: For all ages.

Exception: Children with visual impairment.

Materials: Cardboard rolls (from toilet tissue or paper towels), colored markers or paint and paintbrushes.

Objectives: Body control, breathing awareness and control, socialization.

The game

Players each have one cardboard roll in front of them. They start by painting or coloring an attractive design on the roll. If the group is too large, subdivide into teams of six to ten players depending on the size of the activity room. A race is organized. Each player must roll the cardboard roll to the finish line only by blowing on it, without using his hands. The first to cross the finish line is the winner.

The game ends when all players understand the blowing process.

Note: Each player must cross the finish line in whatever amount of time is needed (other players are asked to encourage any player having difficulties).

73

The Paper Ball Race

Age: For all ages.

Exception: Children with visual impairment.

Materials: Lightweight paper, table (or other elevated surface).

Objectives: Body control, breathing awareness and control, socialization.

The game

Each player is asked to make a small paper ball approximately 2 inches (5 centimeters) in diameter. A race is organized between two to four players at a time. The player places the paper ball on the edge of the table. The aim of this game is to blow the ball across the table as quickly as possible without the ball falling on the floor. The first one to reach the other side is the winner.

The game ends when all players can control their blowing.

Variation: The aim of the game is to blow the ball in the slowest way possible; the player who can move the ball for the longest time while constantly keeping the ball in motion, before it reaches the other side of the table, is the winner.

74

The Spaceship

Age: For very young players.

Exception: None.

Materials: None.

Objectives: Voice development, association of movement with sound, breathing, freedom of intensity, release of anxiety.

The game

The player starts by crouching and using a low voice. While slowly standing, the player must raise the pitch and intensity of his voice. The player then stretches his arms and hands as high as possible with his voice as high and loud as possible. Then his voice slowly comes back down again while gradually lowering body, pitch and intensity.

The game ends after repeating a few times.

Part VI
Creative Thinking

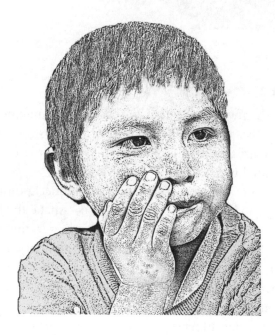

75

Follow the Instructions

Age: For all players.

Exception: Children with visual impairment.

Materials: Pencil, paper, musical instruments.

Objectives: Observation, self-control, socialization, improvement of reading skills, imagination.

The game

A path is established within the activity room, with a number of checkpoints. Each checkpoint has a special instruction, which must be carried out by the player passing it. Instructions can be written in words to improve reading skills, or represented by pictures.

For example, checkpoint 1—play the drum; checkpoint 2—clap hands; checkpoint 3—jump like a rabbit; checkpoint 4—shake the bell. The number of checkpoints is determined by the leader according to the number of players (between five and ten checkpoints is the average number). A player should be stationed at each checkpoint in order to verify that the instruction is properly carried out. Players are lined up behind one another. When the first player reaches checkpoint 3, the second player makes his way to checkpoint 1.

The game ends when all have gone around the course (including players on guard at the checkpoints).

76

I Remember the Singer

Age: For all ages.

Exception: None.

Materials: Pencil and paper.

Objectives: Socialization, memory, acquisition of knowledge.

The game

The group is divided into two teams. Each player thinks of the name of a popular singer (they must all be different). One player asks the other team if they have thought of a particular singer. If yes, the person who thought of that singer changes team. If not, the interviewer changes team.

The game ends when one team has absorbed all players from the other team.

Variation 1: This game can be played with composers.

Variation 2: This game can be played with musical instruments.

Variation 3: This game can be played with animals.

Variation 4: This game can be played with objects found in the activity room.

77

Make Your Own Musical Instrument

Age: For all ages.

Exception: None.

Materials: Paper, cardboard, scissors, strings/rope, crayons, rubber bands, magazine photos, paint and paintbrushes (optional).

Objectives: Imagination, creativity, sound exploration, coordination.

The game

Each player makes a simple musical instrument with ordinary materials (e.g. paper, shoe boxes, elastics, string, baskets, egg boxes, toilet roll tubes, aluminum plates and foil, leaves, wood, stones, shells). The instrument is then decorated with paint, collage, etc.

The activity can be done in the activity room or outdoors, with each location offering different challenges.

The game ends when the instruments are presented and played.

78

Story with Sounds/Story of Sounds

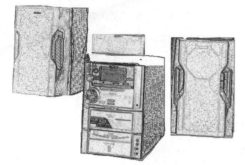

Age: For all ages.

Exception: Children with hearing impairment.

Materials: CD player/recorder, blank CDs.

Objectives: Creativity, sound awareness, self-control, differentiation between fiction and reality, socialization, associative thinking, role playing.

The game

The leader tells a story (for the very young) or asks the players to invent a story and make all the sounds according to the situations occurring in it. They tell the story along with the sounds.

Then the players are asked to tell the story without any words, only with the sounds, which should represent the story. The story is recorded and then listened to by the group.

The game ends after the group discusses the results and the appropriateness of the sounds.

79

Birth of a Butterfly

Age: For younger players.

Exception: None.

Materials: Large piece of cloth, paper, colored pencils and/or crayons.

Objectives: Awareness of development stages, locomotion, creativity, socialization, associative thinking.

The game

Teams of three to four players invent and draw the story of a caterpillar that becomes a butterfly. The players then present their story through a play and/or a dance. Their play or dance must correspond to the drawing.

The game ends after each team has presented its play or dance.

Variation 1: Presentation with voice only.

Variation 2: Presentation without words, just sounds.

Variation 3: Presentation with neither voice nor sounds, just movement.

Variation 4: Presentation with music.

80

Contemporary Music or Drawing Music

Age: For all ages (can be adapted to different age groups).

Exception: Can be adapted for children with hearing or visual impairment.

Materials: Colored pencils, large sheets of paper, different musical instruments.

Objectives: Creativity, organization, decision making, interpretation, eye/movement coordination, socialization, associative thinking.

The game

The group is divided into teams of three to five players. The players invent a song or musical composition using their own personal musical notation system or drawing. They then present their composition along with the visual presentation of their "system" or drawing by playing on one or several musical instruments. They should be able to explain the relationship between their "system" and the music they have played.

The game ends after each team has explained its composition.

Variation: Players are asked to interpret how they perceive another group's composition/drawing.

Note 1: Children with a hearing impairment can use high vibration instruments such as drums and triangles to present a percussion composition.

Note 2: Children with a visual impairment can use string and glue to write out their composition, which they can then interpret on an instrument of their choice.

81

Drawing a Dance

Age: For all ages.

Exception: Children with visual impairment.

Materials: Paper, colored pencils or crayons.

Objectives: Creativity, organization, decision making, musical knowledge (for older players), associative thinking, socialization, interpretation.

The game

The group is asked to work in teams of two or three. Each team makes a drawing of a dance, which can include a story. Each team then presents its dance through choreography and explains the relationship between the drawing and the dance.

The game ends after each team has explained its dance.

Variation: Another team is asked to interpret the drawing.

82

Dramatic Expression

Age: For all ages.

Exception: None.

Materials: CD player, music CDs.

Objectives: Creativity, control of sound and silence to develop the ability to transfer knowledge, socialization, communication, creativity, rhythm, associative thinking, role playing.

The game

In teams of four to six, players invent a story (theatre) about five minutes in length. The leader places the players in a situation such as, "You are in the woods, and suddenly, *something happens*." Each team presents its play using voice, speech, noise, etc. Each team then presents the same play, but this time with no sounds. Then each team reviews the music CDs available in the activity room and selects the one with the most appropriate music for its play. They then present the same play again but this time in rhythm with the music, as in a music video.

The game ends after each team has presented its play as a music video.

Note: Players should already know many of the musical pieces available before selecting the music.

83

What Is the Music Saying?

Age: For all ages.

Exception: Children with hearing impairment.

Materials: CD player, music CDs.

Objectives: Listening, rhythm, creativity, accepting other opinions, listening to different types of music, active listening, associative thinking.

The game

In teams of four to five, players listen to a piece of music and create a story or a play that corresponds to the music. Approximately 10 to 15 minutes are generally needed to prepare. The music and its rhythm must always be followed.

The game ends after each team has presented its story with the music.

Variation: Players are asked to draw the story that they are hearing. They then exchange their drawing with another team. Each team presents its own interpretation of that story.

84

Hold Your Rhythm

Age: For older players.

Exception: Children with hearing impairment.

Materials: Rhythm sticks (claves), stopwatch.

Objectives: Listening, rhythm, consistency, concentration, creativity, socialization, coordination.

The game

The group is divided into two teams. Each player holds two rhythmic sticks. The first team decides on a rhythmic pattern (two or four beats) and starts playing it. On the count of one, the stopwatch is started and the second team must try to catch the rhythm (to start playing the same rhythm as the first team at the exact same time).

Once all members of the second team are playing the exact same rhythm at the exact same time, the leader stops the watch and checks the time.

Roles are then reversed, with the second team starting the rhythm and the first team trying to catch them. Again, the leader checks the time with the stopwatch. The winning team is the one that takes the least time to catch the other team.

The game ends after each team has had a chance to invent a few rhythmic patterns.

Variation: Two players sit face to face with rhythm sticks. One plays a rhythmic pattern (two or four beats), and the other tries to confuse him. After two minutes, if the other player hasn't managed to confuse him, the first player is the winner. They then switch roles. It can be played in teams (only two players confronting at one time).

85

Show Me Your Mood

Age: For all ages.

Exception: None.

Materials: Xylophone, other melodic musical instrument.

Objectives: Creativity, socialization, expression, discussion, analysis of why.

The game

One player is asked to play on the xylophone, in whatever mood he is feeling (e.g. happy, angry, sad, shy). The other players try to guess the emotion. The player who guesses correctly will in turn play the mood he chooses. The leader uses this opportunity to discuss with the team the reason why the player is happy, sad, angry, etc.

The game ends when all players have had a chance to show their mood.

86

I Won't Laugh

Age: For all ages.

Exception: Children with visual impairment.

Materials: None.

Objectives: Creativity, self-control, relaxation.

The game

All sitting together, one player tries to make the others laugh by making funny movements (no talking). The others must look at the entertainer. When a player laughs, he is out. The last player to remain in wins and becomes the entertainer.

The game ends when every player has had a chance to be the entertainer.

87

Creatures from Another Planet

Age: For younger players.

Exception: Can be adapted for children with visual impairment.

Materials: Paper, colored pencils or crayons.

Objectives: Creativity, imagination, awareness of differences between creatures, socialization.

The game

In teams of two or three, players are told that they are going on a trip to another planet. When they get there, they see creatures that are partly similar to yet different from those of earth. They combine scales, feathers and fur. Players must draw one of these animals and determine what sounds it makes and how it moves.

The game ends when every player has presented his creature from another planet to the group.

Note: Children with a visual impairment can use paper, cotton, feathers or any other available materials with glue to create a collage creature.

88

I Am a Sculptor

Age: For all players over six years of age.

Exception: None.

Materials: None.

Objectives: Imagination, creativity, socialization.

The game

In teams of two, one player (the sculptor) models the other (the clay) in an original way. The clay player must keep his arms, body and legs in the position that the sculptor has placed them. After a few minutes, the leader announces the end; the players look at everybody's sculptures and briefly discuss the interesting poses. They then change roles.

The game ends after each player has had a few turns at being a sculptor and the clay.

89

The Alphabet

Age: For younger players.

Exception: None.

Materials: Alphabet cards.

Objectives: Creativity, learning the alphabet, improved reading and writing skills, body movement control, consciousness.

The game

A player selects a letter from a deck of alphabet cards and secretly memorizes it. The player then tries to use his body to show the others which letter it is. The player who guesses the correct letter in turn picks a card and demonstrates the letter with his body.

The game ends when every player has had a chance to demonstrate at least one letter to the others.

90

Create a Music Video

Age: For older players.

Exception: Children with visual impairment.

Materials: Video equipment, selection of music.

Objectives: Creativity, organization, participation, socialization, structure, building self-image, self-confidence, role playing.

The game

In teams of three to six, a topic for a video is chosen along with appropriate music. The team must act along to the music without any words; imitating a singer within a story is permitted. Players must follow the beat of the music at *all times*. This is similar to popular music videos and therefore players will be familiar with the idea.

The leader films the players in action. All music videos are then watched and commented on by the players.

The game ends after each team has presented its music video.

Note: If the movements do not match the music, or if there is too much violence or inappropriate behavior in the video, the leader must get the players to realize and admit that the video was badly prepared, and that they should redo the video to correspond to the music. The group can then review the first and second videos and discuss the difference in outcome in order to reinforce positive behavior. It is necessary that the change in behavior comes *from the players* and that it is not forced on them by the leader. Players must never end this game feeling they have failed.

Part VII
Relaxation

91

Tin Soldier/Rag Doll

Age: For all ages (must be adapted for older players).

Exception: None.

Materials: None.

Objectives: Body parts control, discrimination, socialization, contraction, relaxation.

The game

Players are asked to stand up straight and stiff as if they were little tin soldiers. The leader goes around and checks all the players to see if they are very stiff; the leader encourages them to become even more rigid. When the leader says the words "rag doll," all players drop on the floor and pretend they are made out of rags. The leader then goes around and checks the softness and relaxation of each player; the leader must shake the arms and legs of the players to make sure they are like rags. The leader then announces "tin soldier" and all players quickly get up and stand straight and stiff again.

The game ends after repeating a few times.

Variation: For older players, play as above except replace the words "tin soldier" with the sound of an instrument such as a drum, and the words "rag doll" with the sound of a contrasting instrument such as a triangle.

92

Kaboom!

Age: For all ages.

Exception: None.

Materials: None.

Objectives: Breathing control, physical release through voice, socialization, relaxation.

The game

Players lie on the floor. They are all deflated balloons. The leader asks the players to inflate the balloon, which they do by inhaling more and more air into their tummies. When the leader announces that the balloons are full, the players yell "KABOOM!" and pretend their bodies are deflating like an untied balloon that has been released. They move around the room until the "balloon" lies on the floor again, totally deflated and motionless.

The game ends after repeating a few times.

93

Ghosts

Age: For younger players.

Exception: None.

Materials: None.

Objectives: Body movement control, patience, socialization, relaxation.

The game

Players lie on the floor. They know that ghosts only come out at night. When all players have stopped moving, the leader turns off the lights (there must always be a little light in the activity room). The leader then touches the player who was the first to stop moving completely; the player then gets up imitating the sound of a ghost (whooooo…), moving around the room and around the other players. This little ghost touches another player who gets up and goes to touch yet another player. When all the little ghosts are floating around the room, the leader turns on the light and all the ghosts fall on the floor, remaining the way they are when they fall, totally motionless. The game begins again.

The game ends after repeating a few times.

94

Cooking Spaghetti

Age: For younger players.

Exception: None.

Materials: None.

Objectives: Body control, socialization, relaxation.

The game

All players lie on the floor. They are like uncooked spaghetti: very straight and hard, and closely packed one against the other. The leader tells the spaghetti players that the water is getting warmer and therefore the spaghetti is becoming softer, starting to bend at the end. It then bends more and more until the spaghetti starts intertwining with other spaghetti. Players must follow directions and will generally finish all mixed together, piled up one over the other.

The game ends after repeating a few times.

95

Sizzling Bacon

Age: For younger players.

Exception: None.

Materials: None.

Objectives: Body control, relaxation.

The game

Each player is like a slice of bacon lying very flat and motionless on the floor. The leader tells the players that they are now being fried; the leader will explain that the bacon is slowly starting to sizzle, sometimes with small bursts. The bacon is wiggling more and more until properly cooked. The players should follow the movements with their body.

The game ends after repeating a few times.

96

The Gingerbread Cookies

Age: For all ages.

Exception: None (may need to be adapted for children with a physical disability).

Materials: None.

Objectives: Relaxation, socialization, body control, trust in peers, development.

The game

Each player is the gingerbread dough. The player is soft and can be manipulated easily. The leader will touch each of the players in order to check if they are relaxed, moving their arms and legs. The leader then announces that he is baking the cookies. The players are now thin and crispy and cannot bend. The leader then lifts each player by holding and raising him from the shoulders. The player must stay perfectly straight and not bend or move to get on his feet. The player must learn to trust the leader enough to be lifted from the shoulders as straight as a cookie.

The game ends after repeating a few times.

Note: For children with a physical disability that prevents them from standing easily, the leader could turn them like cookies in a cookie pan, or move them on the floor by pulling, making sure that the child stays as stiff as a crispy cookie.

97

The Bomb

Age: For very young players.

Exception: None.

Materials: None.

Objectives: Body awareness, self-awareness, exteriorization, relaxation.

The game

Players are on the floor, curled up in a little ball. Then the countdown begins: 10–9–8–7–6–5–4–3–2–1, BOOOOOM. The bomb explodes and the players yell the sound of the explosion with their bodies jumping in the air. They then fall on their backs, motionless. The leader should make sure that the bodies of all players are totally relaxed and still.

The game ends after repeating a few times.

98

The Flying Handkerchief

Age: For all ages.

Exception: None.

Materials: Facial tissues (or a light handkerchief for each player).

Objectives: Self-awareness, breathing control, relaxation.

The game

Players are lying on the floor. The leader places one facial tissue on the face of each player. Each player is then asked to blow the tissue into the air as high as possible.

The game ends when every player is able to keep the tissue in the air for a few seconds.

Variation: Players are standing up. They must blow the tissue and keep it in the air as long as possible.

99

The Very Little Engine

Age: For younger players.

Exception: None.

Materials: None.

Objectives: Relaxation, body control, breathing control, speech improvement.

The game

Players are sitting on the floor. They are told that each one of them is a little engine inside of a car or motorcycle, for which the fuel is "air." Players are asked to breathe in, and, as they breathe out, to produce the sound of an engine (vroooom); the engine stops when there is no more fuel (air). The aim of this game is to see who has the most economical engine—the player that sounds the longest without taking a second breath. Players are expected to move around while the engine is running, and fall on the floor when it is out of fuel.

The game ends after repeating a few times.

Note: The leader should make sure that the players are breathing normally and calmly when they fall on the floor.

100

Scarf Dancing

Age: For all ages.

Exception: None.

Materials: Scarves, music CDs.

Objectives: Flowing movement, relaxation.

The game

Players dance with scarves while beautiful flowing music plays. This encourages graceful movements and relaxation.

The game ends after approximately five to seven minutes, which should allow every player to feel relaxed and start flowing with the music.